CHRONICLES

OF THE

UNKNOWN DREAMER

2013

JEREMIAH JOHNSON

Cover design by Sandra L. Burdine
Edited by Allyson Hurndon

To order copies of this book and other products from Jeremiah Johnson in
bulk quantities, please contact us at 863-940-2867 or visit our website at
www.chroniclesoftheunknowndreamer.com.

DISCLAIMER

Do not become obsessed with the following dreams and revelations. The words contained in this book are intended to lead you into a pursuit and personal encounter with the person of Jesus Christ through His written Word. May we keep our eyes fixed upon Him and Him alone in this hour!

CONTENTS

Foreword by R. Loren Sandford...xi

Introduction:..xv

1. November 2011:
   The Perfect Storm...1

   The Sleeping Church..3
   The Street Church...4
   The Surrendered Church..7

2. November 6, 2012:
   Regarding the Election and Future of America.................9

3. November 15, 2012:
   The Next Four Years in America..................................11

   Five Key Areas that the Church Must Change its Position On:

      Abortion...14
      Sexual Immorality...18
      Tolerance and Rebellion.......................................19
      Hillary Clinton..22
      Israel..23

      Syria...25
      Mongoloid in the South..26

4. December 15, 2012:
   Sandy Hook Elementary Shootings..............................29

5. January 4, 2013:
   The Black Plague Coming to the School Systems.............33

6. January 24, 2013:
   Shots Fired at the White House....................................35

7. **February 21, 2013:**
    A Generation of Jobs and Josephs...................................39

8. **March 20, 2013:**
    The Heart of the Father...41

9. **April 6, 2013:**
    Visitation from Jesus Christ..43

10. **April 17, 2013:**
    The Prophet's Bread...47

11. **April 25, 2013:**
    Life Dream for Central Florida......................................49

12. **April 27, 2013:**
    The Deceived Church...51

13. **May 1, 2013:**
    Terrorist Network Coming to the United States.............53

14. **May 7, 2013:**
    The Eagle Has Landed..55

15. **May 30, 2013:**
    Hell is for Real..59

16. **June 20, 2013:**
    The Days of King Hezekiah: A Warning About President
    Obama...63

17. **June 6, 2013:**
    Rent a Ministry...67

18. **September 15, 2013:**
    A Warning to the Signs and Wonders Movement............71

19. **October 15, 2013:**
    A Warning to the Prophets and Prophetic Movement..........75

Prophetic Word for 2014..79

20. Preparation in the Midst of Uncertainty...............................81

      The Rise and Fall of Ministers....................................83
      Increasingly Disoriented Weather Patterns........................85
      Washington D.C. on High Alert..86
      China- The Sleeping Giant Will Awake.............................87

Dreams for the Days Ahead...89

21. The Rise of Obadiah's Prophets......................................91

22. A Culture Driven by Hate...93

23. Homosexual and Muslim Influence in the Military.................95

ACKNOWLEDGMENTS

Thank you Abba Father for granting me access into the deep places of your heart since I was a little boy. I am most grateful to share with others what the Holy Spirit reveals to me as I sleep at night.

Thank you to my father Joseph, who paid a great price to create a spiritual atmosphere of freedom and release that fostered the gift of prophecy in my life since the days of my youth.

Thank you to my mother, Sandra, for consistently encouraging me to pursue my dreams and never look back.

Thank you to my dear Uncle Chris who has been both an instrument of encouragement and correction in my life. Your love for the Scriptures and faithful challenges to me over the years have impacted my life more than words can express.

Thank you to Peter and Nancy McFarlane for making the distribution of this book possible. Great is your reward in heaven! You both are so dear to my heart.

Thank you to Allyson Hurndon for your countless hours of editing. Your perspective and kind words have helped to encourage me to finish this work that the Father has started.

A special love and thanks to my dear wife and best friend Morgan Leah. Only one person knows what it's like to sleep next to a dreamer like me, and that's you! How many times have you asked me, "What in the world were you dreaming about last night?" and we laugh together. Thank you for being my calm in the midst of the storms and an ever-increasing source of beauty and mystery. I love you with all of my heart.

FOREWORD

Prophetic people come in a variety of "packages." Some function as what Bob Jones calls "Nathan prophets." In their oneness with the Father's heart, they just know things deep in their spirit without much mysticism attached to the knowing. Others have the seer's gift. These experience visions of various sorts, both mental images and open visions manifesting as in the natural. Still others, like Joseph the son of Jacob, are dreamers and interpreters of dreams. Among other things, Jeremiah Johnson is a dreamer.

In Scripture God gave symbolic dreams needing interpretation to unbelievers and outsiders but, more often than not, dreams given to His own needed little if any interpretation. Obviously, this is not a hard and fast rule, but it can be seen to be generally true. Witness, for instance, the dream given to Jesus' foster father, Joseph, telling him to go to Egypt to escape Pharaoh's murderous intent. The dream that followed was equally clear, telling him to return because Herod had died. Neither dream contained any symbolism or mystery needing interpretation.

Today it seems that the wilder and more mysterious the symbolism of a dream, the more spiritual the body of Christ thinks the recipient is. I, however, see it the other way around. God would much rather speak to us clearly and directly through our dreams and visions, but because of our spiritual and relational dysfunction He often cannot. Jeremiah's dreams bear the mark of direct revelation with little symbolism to cloud the issues or allow for differing interpretations.

As an older prophetic voice, I recognize in Jeremiah the calling of a younger generation of leaders and prophetic voices just now emerging, unafraid to stand under and learn from those of us who have gone before. Godly humility is their hallmark, and passionate love for Jesus is their motivation. Some of us saw them coming years ago, and now they begin to manifest.

Unlike so many others of their generation, these young leaders bear a deep concern for accurately representing the Father's heart to a fatherless generation, for lives conformed to the image of the Son and for attracting no glory to themselves. In that spirit Jeremiah has presented prophecies for the coming days that reflect much of what I myself have seen. I can confirm their accuracy. These prophetic words come in two categories, both of which have ample scriptural precedent.

Category 1: The prophetic word prepares the body of Christ for the coming days. In the Book of Acts Agabus prophesied a coming famine and thus helped the body of Christ to begin to prepare. Similarly, he warned Paul that if he went to Jerusalem he would be arrested. Paul went anyway, but he went prepared for the ordeal he would ultimately face. Some of Jeremiah's prophecies serve this preparatory purpose, warning of what is to come that we might ready ourselves to be effective in ministry in a darkening day.

Category 2: Jeremiah's Old Testament namesake received his prophetic call at a very young age with a commission to "pluck up and to break down, To destroy and to overthrow, To build and to plant" (Jeremiah 1:10). As did

Elijah before him, with his words Jeremiah tore down and uprooted what was impure in the life and devotion of Israel and sought to establish or plant that which was good and righteous. In our day, God cries out for a purified bride to shine in the midst of a culture collapsing under the weight of its own sin and defilement. Prophetic people who understand the times raise their voices on behalf of a righteous God to separate the precious from the vile and restore glory to His people and to His name.

This small book of dreams accomplishes both of these purposes. Jeremiah speaks directly and strongly to issues that can only be addressed with a powerful and uncompromising voice, both preparing and confronting the Church in love that she might rise to the high calling of God in this hour. Take what he says very seriously.

R. Loren Sandford
November 2013

Jeremiah Johnson

INTRODUCTION

It all began one night when I was twelve years old. I was sitting on the front pew of a church that my father was co-pastoring. This particular night, a prophet from Arkansas was in town, and as he was ministering he turned to me and said,

" *'And you son, you will have a very unusual ministry. You will write down the dreams and visions that God gives you, and you will put them into print. You will prophesy to the nations and tear down and uproot that which is built upon carnal foundations and structures,' says the Lord.* "

I remember receiving my first dream from the Lord that very night. After that, the dreams just came. They started coming so frequently as a child that I began to sleep with a tape recorder by the side of my bed. Upon waking up from a dream, I would speak out everything that I had seen and heard, taking note of the specific details. Over the years as I continued this process, I began to have almost total recall of what had taken place in my dreams.

A few years after this momentous night in my life, my mother would reveal to me what the Lord had spoken to her while I was in her womb. I was to be given the name Jeremiah, and I was to be a prophet, one who dreamed dreams and prophesied to nations.

Many nights I awaken out of breath, exhausted, and alarmed to very literal and weighty revelations from the Father given to me as I sleep. Being a man mostly concerned with the well being of my family and the shepherding of a small church in Lakeland, Florida, I have often wondered why the Father would grant me access to the details of His heart in regard to the destinies of nations. Or why I, one who has very little interest in politics, would be given dreams concerning the detrimental consequences of elections and world movements. I am truly humbled at the responsibility of this gift I carry, and in many ways these entries are a releasing of the burden I bear on a daily basis.

The book that you hold in your hands is a fulfillment not only of the obedience of the prophet from Arkansas but my mother who was faithful to follow the direction of a dream from the Lord. Please note that there is no intended connection between the dreams shared in each chapter, but similar themes, messages, and words of prophecy weave their way throughout the book's entirety. The dreams contained in this book were received between November 2012 to November 2013. The first chapter begins with a fulfillment of a dream I had in November of 2011 that came to pass in November of 2012. The last chapter in the book contains specific prophecies for the year 2014 and finishes with some dreams that stretch beyond 2014.

I encourage you to find a quiet place and sit down. Push away the distractions and open up your heart to hear what the Spirit is saying in this hour. As you read, I believe you will begin to feel the tangible and unmistakable burden that can only come from the Spirit of God. May this book be used to encourage, correct, and warn the body of Christ. I pray that intercessors would rejoice at the specific assignments being released throughout these pages. True prophecy will always give us a prayer agenda.

I'm yours in Jesus Christ,

Jeremiah Johnson

Jeremiah Johnson

—————————————

CHRONICLES

OF THE

UNKNOWN DREAMER

2013

—————————————

Jeremiah Johnson

1

November 2011

THE PERFECT STORM

On October 29, 2012, Hurricane Sandy made an unexpected sharp turn toward the Northeast coast of the United States on a path toward the shores of New Jersey.

As many Americans began to recognize the physical devastation that was inevitable, I was personally experiencing something quite different. A deep suffocating feeling of emotion and pain came over my soul as tears filled my eyes. I knew what Hurricane Sandy was bringing to the shores of the United States, and it was deeply troubling. This massive storm wasn't just a sign of physical disaster. It was a spiritual plague descending upon our nation.

In November of 2011, just one year before Hurricane Sandy hit the Northeast coast of the United States, I awoke from one of the most incredibly detailed dreams of my life. Immediately I sensed the urgency of its message and wrote it down and published it. I told people that what I saw would happen within one year's time.

In the dream, I found myself standing on the shoreline of the Atlantic coast facing the ocean. There was a tremendous storm front that was beginning to gather in the Atlantic. I could see the tip of Florida to my right and the upper parts of Maine to my left. I had a sense that I was somewhere near or in Virginia.

As I looked up over the Atlantic Ocean, I noticed two enormous storms beginning to form. The first front moved ahead of the other. The Spirit of God spoke to me and said, *"The Perfect Storm is upon America."* These two fronts immediately began to move toward me, and demons began to manifest inside of them. I called out to the first front sweeping toward me and said, "Who are you?" The word "**Rebellion**" flashed before my eyes. I called out to the front behind it and said, "Who are you?" The word "**Tolerance**" appeared in the sky.

As these tremendous storms now passed over my head, I violently cried out and said, "I live in the most rebellious and tolerant generation that the world has ever known." The Spirit of God responded to me and said,

"The former prophets looked for physical storms by which they saw my judgments coming, but in these days I'm raising up prophets that will discern spiritual storms. You must know that the spiritual storms that are upon the earth are far greater than any physical storm that has touched Earth. Physical storms are limited to a region of people. These spiritual

storms that shall rise in the earth will have the power to affect every area of culture. Beware!"

As I faced America on the Atlantic coast and saw these two massive storms sweeping the land, I felt a tremendous urgency of the hour. I immediately jumped on a horse and began to ride, and the word "Paul Revere" was placed in my mouth as I rode. During the next years in the dream, I traveled to different churches all over America proclaiming what I had seen and heard.

Though I went to several different churches and visited many different ethnic groups all over America, there were only three categories of churches. The following are the encounters that I had as I visited the different churches:

THE SLEEPING CHURCH

The first type of church I visited had "Sleeping Church" engraved on its doors. As I opened the doors to these churches, every one of them was in the middle of a service. I would hurry in to relay the message of what I had just seen and heard, only to be shocked to see everyone in attendance, including the leadership, sucking on pacifiers. While this type of church could hear my words, they had no ability to respond. I began to cry out and say, "Why are you silent, Church, why are you silent? Though you are awake, you are sleeping!"

In the dream, the Holy Spirit immediately spoke to me Eph 4:14, *"Then we will no longer be infants, tossed back and forth by the waves, and blown here and there by every wind of teaching and by the cunning and craftiness of men in their deceitful scheming."*

THE STREET CHURCH

The second type of church I visited met in the streets of America. Upon seeing all of these different gatherings in many different cities, I was delighted because many of them seemed to be around my age (18-35) and simply claimed allegiance to "Street Church." I began to interview and ask members of this particular type of church if they had heard about the two storms descending over America named "Rebellion" and "Tolerance." None of them seemed to understand what I was asking.

I continued in the street on my horse until I found myself at a gathering of thousands and thousands of these "Street Church" people. I recognized one of the leaders, but for the sake of integrity I will leave his name out. As I pressed into the crowd, there was an incredible sense of chaos and confusion among the people. I cried out to the Lord in the dream and said, "Who are these people?"

He said, *"These are the products of the works-based gospel movement of the 80s and 90s. These are they that have rebelled in the name of grace but not in the name of My Son."* As the Spirit spoke this to me, there began to be mass commotion in the crowd.

Suddenly, banners began to be carried by the Street Church all over America that read "GRACE." It was especially intriguing to me that these banners were dusty, and you could visibly see the mud on them. I said to the Lord, "Where have these young people picked up these banners from?" He said, *"They have resurrected them from the former generations. False doctrines that were once done away with are now rising in the streets."* The Spirit specifically showed me three false doctrines these groups believed in. They were:

1. ***Manifest Sons of God Doctrine***

2. ***Joel's Army***

3. ***Finished Work of the Cross Movement***

SPECIFICS OF THESE DOCTRINES

Manifest Sons of God Doctrine

Those that resurrect this teaching will specifically focus on the perfection of the saints, immortalization, and the attainment of actually being Christ as we become just like Him in nature and ability. This doctrine, as stated in the dream, will be carried by thousands of young adults being deceived because of the lack of biblical literacy and false teachers leading them astray.

Joel's Army Doctrine

This doctrine will specifically be marked by those who believe that the Church has replaced Israel. This is also known as Replacement Theology. Dominion Theology and claims of divinity will also mark those who follow this doctrine.

Finished Work of the Cross Doctrine

I am aware that many people have never heard of this doctrine or movement that is really beginning to deceive many young people. In all my research and study, burned-out young people that have served God through striving and never understood grace are the primary targets of this deceptive doctrine and movement. The problem with the movement and doctrine is that while there is much truth in the teaching that Christ is our final sacrifice, this movement believes that all mankind has been reconciled to God, which is universalism. Postmodern universalists believe that unrepentant individuals will go to hell but upon going there will recognize their sin and ultimately be taken to heaven. This movement teaches that because Christ was sacrificed once and for all, Christians will never have to make sacrifices.

He showed me that these three doctrines would begin to creep into the church because of the lack of biblical knowledge coupled with tolerance and rebellion. I began to follow the grace banners with the people to the cities where they went. As the Street Church swarmed the crowds, they pulled out mace from their pockets. They began to spray people in the eyes and the Spirit said,

"They are blinding the generations to the truth in the name of grace. They call themselves Joel's army because they believe they will usher in the last day's grace movement in the earth, but know that they are like the locust seeking to devour and ravage the vineyards of young generations. They distort the truth and preach rebellion and tolerance in the name of grace. They shall question if hell exists. They will believe that many paths lead to Me. Their toleration has led to jubilation. They create crazy party atmospheres that attract the drug culture and the homosexual spirit. You must know that things are never as they appear with the Street Church."

After visiting these two types of churches, I was in great distress. I cried out to the Spirit and said, "Take me to Your church." I immediately rode up on a church building that had "Surrendered Church" on its doors.

THE SURRENDERED CHURCH

I quickly walked in and sat down. I immediately noticed that in the back of this church was a gaping hole. It was as if a blast had gone off and almost entirely knocked out the back walls of the Surrendered Church. As I visited surrendered churches all over America, I found the exact same thing. I sat in the back and asked the Father what had happened. He said, *"My church was at first deceived by rebellion and tolerance. The Street Church you just saw stormed out of the back of My church and left because of the lack of foundation and character, but now My church has been awakened and shall be repaired."*

7

I got up out of my seat and watched as many people were working on repairing the gaping hole in the back of the church. As I watched, I noticed something interesting; the workers were not just any workers. They were true apostles and prophets restoring the foundation, and many of them were teaching other young men how to properly lay the foundation. Meanwhile, many intercessors were in great travail repenting but having a great sense of hope as they cried out and thanked the Father for awakening His Son's bride from deception and for restoring the foundation layers to His church.

The Perfect Storm has landed in America right around election time as prophesied in November 2011. Rebellion and Tolerance have swept over our land. Three different types of churches are on every street corner in America. Will the Surrendered Church arise and take its rightful place amongst the masses? I believe it can and must do so in this hour.

2

November 6, 2012

REGARDING THE ELECTION AND FUTURE OF AMERICA

There was a large group that had gathered where I was speaking. I took the podium and told them of an incredible dream that I had in which the Lord had spoken to me about the election and the destiny of America. This is what I prophesied to the crowd gathered:

"The destiny of America is not found in our ability to vote today but in our ability to put our faith in the God that will move mountains. Do not be surprised in 2013 at the complaining and murmuring that will arise in America regarding the President of the United States. The labor pains are going to greatly increase all over the earth. There will be wars and many rumors of war. Natural disasters and exceedingly great complications will take place on American soil and in the Middle East. But behold, Jehovah will make Himself known as never before. Yes, the voice of the American people in the years to come will turn from complaining, murmuring, outrage, and fear to one of rejoicing over the goodness of God being displayed in their midst. The word "scandal" is going to become a household name. As millions watch the voter count, even tonight, scandals and controversy will bring chaos and confusion. Many acts of betrayal and fraud will rise among agencies and governments. Dictators will be overthrown. Public policy will be under the microscope like never before. This will be a sign to you that truth must win the day in the home and in government. The state of America shall be likened unto the state of Israel in the book of Exodus. 'I see China as Egypt,' says the Lord. 'They will attempt to chase down America in the years to come through trade and the free market. At first their attitude will be peace and tranquility, but then a tightening, a hardening heart, will bring much trouble economically to America. There is one besides China that will rise and greatly assist America in times of economic trouble. Do not be afraid. I am even now channeling resources in different countries to assist the American economy in the years to come. Do not be so foolish as to rely on China for everything. Are they God? Do I have an equal? Trust in Me,' says your God."

Then I awoke.

3

November 15, 2012

THE NEXT FOUR YEARS IN AMERICA

After President Obama's victory in the 2012 election, I began to pray for heaven's perspective on what took place. I have found that the key to bringing forth prophetic words that are pure and unadulterated is to pray into the perspective of the Father and to release His words.

I went to sleep on Thursday, November 15, 2012, and had a very powerful dream. Heaven's perspective on the election was not only given to me but also a very clear picture of the next four years in the United States and prophetic words for several foreign nations.

In the dream, I found myself walking all over the United States. In every city I visited, I constantly heard the sound of a woman in labor. Cities all over the United States were underneath hospitals that had been built over them. All that I could hear were these women's labor cries. They were groaning with tremendous pain and longing to see their children. I had a sense that this was their firstborn and that they had never conceived before. The anticipation and expectancy could be felt in every city in America.

Suddenly, the voice of the Father echoed over a heavenly speaker from the hospitals built over these cities. The speakers boomed four times, *"Braxton Hicks, Braxton Hicks, Braxton Hicks, Braxton Hicks."*

As the nation heard this proclamation four times, there was a tremendous release. The labor pains ceased. There was silence in every city in America. Then the Father spoke again. This is what He said:

"The 2012 election in the United States was false labor. Though the labor pains increased in every city, I have mercifully granted four more years to the American church to change their position on five key areas that are upon My heart in this hour. The next four years in the United States will be known as the years of "complications." Because I have kept what must be birthed in the United States in the womb for another four years, great complications will mark the pregnancy. What will guarantee the safety of what must be birthed in four years is the American church changing its position on five strategic areas that are upon my heart."

As the Father's declaration was received, those that despised Him cheered and mocked His words, but the American church shook under the weight of His voice.

Thousands of intercessors went into great travail. I noticed a woman on a chariot who began to gather demonic forces. She too had heard the Father's decree. She understood that it would be the intercessors that would shift the American church in their position on the five key areas that the Father said must be dealt with.

This woman is no stranger to me. Her name is Jezebel, and she had visited my city, Lakeland, Florida, in a dream I had years ago. I believe that she plans to visit every city in the United States and will use a similar strategy as she did in my city. She wants to wipe out the intercessory movement in America, and she will do it through pastors and leaders who will tolerate her manipulation and control.

The intercessors in the earth must specifically cover pastors and leaders in prayer over the next four years. They must pray for a backbone in pastors who allow their hearts to grow passive and risk tolerating Jezebel and her ways. It is imperative that the prayer movement begin to develop young intercessors who can carry this burden in the coming years.

Five Key Areas that the Church Must Change its Position On:

As my eyes turned from Jezebel and her demonic forces gathering in the United States, the Father spoke to me privately so that no one could hear Him. He began to share with me the five areas that He is giving the Church four years to change their position on. The following are the five areas that He spoke to me in the dream:

1. ABORTION

The Father spoke to me and said, *"Jeremiah, the primary area that is upon my heart in this hour is the issue of abortion. I have given you a dream that must reach the four corners of the United States. The Church must unify on this issue. I am giving them four years to do it. If they will, a great birthing will take place in 2016."* He then took me to the same factory that I had been to before regarding abortion. He showed me the same dream again. Here is the dream:

Let My Babies Go Dream

I began to walk down a dirt road that I had traveled on in a previous dream, and the Spirit of God said to me, *"I want to show you the cries that come before My throne day and night."*

I walked up to a huge factory where a line of men and women filled the street. The factory was dark and the hair on my body was standing straight up. Most of the women in line, trying to get into the factory, were very pregnant while others of them were carrying small children. As I made my way to the front of the line, I heard screams coming from inside, blood curdling screams. There was an inscription on the top of the door that read "House of Horror." As I walked inside, I realized that this factory was an enormous abortion clinic, and I began to weep. There were hundreds of cribs in this factory, and the floor was about as big as a football field. As I began to look inside the cribs, I saw very small babies with snakes wrapped around them. It was horrifying. I moved from crib to crib watching these snakes choke and kill these babies. I noticed that the women that were dropping these babies off were dejected, defeated, and overwhelmed. I stared into their eyes and pleaded with them, but their minds and hearts were already made up.

All of a sudden, the House of Horror began to shake. It felt like a tremendous earthquake was unearthing the foundation of the factory. Then came a booming, loud, and fatherly voice that said, *"LET MY BABIES GO!!!!"*

At the sound of the Father's voice, I cried out violently and said, "Father what is this? What is this House of Horror? Who are these snakes?" He said to me, *"This House of Horror and houses like this are what have my full attention in this hour. The snakes are the spirits of suicide and death. They are methodically killing off the next generations. The dejected, defeated, and overwhelming look that you see on those women's faces is what happens when they come into agreement with the lies of the Deceiver."*

I left the factory weeping. I was inconsolable. I began saying to the Father, "But I just want to see your house, Papa! I want to see what is inside your factory!" And He said to me, *"So have you asked, so shall I show you."* I turned down a dirt road, and there before me was a glowing factory. It was made of gold and pearls. There were angelic hosts guarding it day and night. There was also a line of people out in front of this factory, just like the House of Horror, except none of the women and men had children, and these women were pregnant. I thought that this was peculiar.

As I approached the entrance to this glowing factory, the Father's factory, before me was a beautiful and radiant inscription that read "House of Hope." As I walked into this factory, I heard laughing, hysterical laughter. I began to look around inside the Hope Factory and realized that the sound was coming from the cribs. I said to the Father, "These babies are too young to laugh like this." He said to me, *"Jeremiah, this is the laugh of the redeemed that no man can contain or deny."*

I began to pay special attention to the babies. I wanted to make sure that there were no snakes in the cribs. As I looked down into all the cribs in the Hope Factory, I noticed that in each and every one of them there was an inscription woven into the crib bed where the babies were lying. The inscriptions read, *"Isaiah 66:9, 'Shall I bring to the point of birth and not give delivery?'* says the LORD. *'Or shall I who gives delivery shut the womb?'* says your God."

I began to shout aloud in the Hope Factory, and I rejoiced over these babies with laughter, dancing, and singing. I joined with these young ones in the "laugh of the redeemed." As I paraded my way around, the Spirit of God spoke to me and said,

"Jeremiah, I want you to tell the people what you have seen and heard. I want you to shout this from the North, to the South, and to the East and the West. Gather my sons and daughters from afar, for I am now raising up the spirit of adoption, specifically amongst my bride. Even as I am bringing many sons and daughters to glory, so I am going to sovereignly begin to place the murder of the innocent at the doorsteps of many many hearts. Houses of Horror will begin to rise in the earth. I hear their cries, Jeremiah. I will not turn My ears and eyes away from My precious ones. Watch the White House. My people will gather there to fight for hope. People from all over the nation will gather to fight for the lives of the innocent ones. Watch and see. There will be many in the earth that will begin to adopt. I am even now championing this cause. I am touching sons and daughters and planting inside of them a heart to adopt from My House of Hope. None of the women and men that you saw lined up outside my House of Hope had children or babies because they were coming to My house to adopt."

As the Father finished speaking to me, I began to find my way to the entrance of the factory. As I walked outside, I thanked everyone in the line. I said, "The Father wants to personally thank you for coming to His House of Hope and championing this cause in the earth, which has come before His throne. He will not watch and wait any longer." I began to notice women in their 50s, 60s, and 70s standing in the back of the line. I said, "Father? Them too?" He said to me,

"Yes, Jeremiah, shall these women not also partake in my invitation to adopt in this hour?" I walked away from the Hope Factory rejoicing but also filled with sadness as I once again noticed the factory of horror that I had walked into earlier that night.

2. SEXUAL IMMORALITY

In the dream, the second area that was on the Father's heart that the Church must change their position on is sexual immorality. He began to show me massive gatherings of homosexuals all over the United States. They formed what were known as colonies where every elected official in the city was gay. He showed me their plots to gain control of the government through their agenda, so that they could affect every area of society.

The Church came out to protest the gathering of homosexuals and their agendas, but then something portentous happened. God the Father began to rebuke the Church saying, *"Has your laziness and blindness on the issue of sexual immorality within the Church not given the homosexual agenda its true power? The issue is not the homosexual agenda. The issue that I have with you is the power that you have given it by failing to preach holiness and purity to masses. I have not called you to persecute homosexuals. I have called you to repent to Me for your wickedness and sin. I will take care of them. You must take care of yourself. Your doctrine is inaccurate. Your motives are impure. Before you pluck the speck out of their eyes, you have plenty in your own."*

The Church began to weep and wail. The sound was ear-piercing. They began to recognize their deception and how immorality had overrun the Church and been accepted rather than dealt with. As repentance took place, the Father spoke again, *"My answer to the homosexual agenda in the earth is a movement of purity. I will gather hundreds of thousands of pure ones that will unite in an effort to confront the issues of their day. It will be internally focused, not externally focused. They will keep their hand to the plow concentrating on immorality within their ranks, and then I will begin to deal with the homosexual agenda on My own terms. There will be new diseases amongst the sexually immoral that will be like a plague. They will reap what they have sown. Science will begin to identify the diseases that will overrun an immoral people in the earth in the years to come."*

3. TOLERANCE AND REBELLION

The third area that the Father showed me the Church must change its position on is our view on love. We must be very careful that loving people is not actually tolerating their rebellion. You will recall the Perfect Storm that I saw descending over America. I want to specifically look at the Street Church because it is a breeding ground for tolerance and rebellion. Below is what the Holy Spirit showed me about this movement:

"They are blinding the generations to the truth in the name of grace. They call themselves Joel's army because they believe they will usher in the last day's grace movement in the earth, but know that they are like the locust seeking to devour and ravage the vineyards of young generations.

They distort the truth and preach rebellion and tolerance in the name of grace. They shall question if hell exists. They will believe that many paths lead to Me. Their toleration has led to jubilation. They create crazy party atmospheres that attract the drug culture and the homosexual spirit. You must know that things are never as they appear with the Street Church."

One of the greatest challenges that the Church in the West is facing and will face is how to deal with young people that have never understood or been taught biblical grace. Many of these people have been overly exposed to legalism and because of this are now embracing false grace. There is a movement in the earth that is targeting young adults, that attracts the drug culture and the homosexual spirit all in the name of love and the finished works of Jesus Christ. Below are two points regarding the deception of tolerance and rebellion:

Tolerance is seeking to silence the voice of truth in America. Seventy-two percent of Americans between the ages of 18-25 reject the notion of absolute truth. America is being governed by moral relativism. This belief states that all values are legitimate, and that it is impossible to judge between them. Truth is reduced to a personal preference, i.e., what's true works for you.

The Penn State scandal is a prophetic word to the Church. This is what will happen when we silence the truth to save face with other people. Moral relativism is attempting to silence the voice of truth in the Church, and we will pay a dear price if we do not begin to speak out.

Abraham Kuyper said, "When principles that run against our greatest convictions begin to win the day, then battle is your calling and **peace** has become your sin. You must at the greatest price, lay your convictions bare before friend and foe, with all the fire of your faith."

Peace has become the great sin of the Christian church in America. In the name of love we have tolerated beliefs and lifestyles that Jesus Christ has never endorsed.

Tolerance is seeking to distort love. Tolerance says, "You must agree with everything I say and do." Love says, " I will tell you the truth because I'm convinced the truth will set you free." To paint Jesus Christ as the God-man who walked the earth and endorsed and accepted all belief systems and lifestyles is a direct assault on the cross. If Jesus tolerated people and their lifestyles, why then did He die on the cross? Was the cross not judgment on unrepentant sinners? "I am the way, the truth, and the life" does not sound like it endorses and tolerates behavior contrary to Scripture. It actually condemns it. If Jesus Christ walked the earth today, He would be considered one of the most intolerant people that ever lived.

There must be a shift in the American church over the next four years with regard to the views of Tolerance and Rebellion. The spirit of truth must be given access to this specific area that is on the Father's heart in this hour.

4. HILLARY CLINTON

The fourth area shown to me in the dream was focused on the American church's perception of Hillary Clinton. I was shown her face in this dream, and then all of a sudden the applause of the nations began to roar as they cried out for her to gain more power in the United States. At this point in the dream, my attention was shifted to the terrorist attack on Benghazi. The Spirit of God began to show me that her hands had a part in the disaster, and He was allowing light to be shed in the dark places as a prophetic word to the Church. The Spirit said to me, *"Take careful notice of the secrecy that she operates in. Beware of what goes on behind the scenes with her. The Church must resist her. She has plans to control, plans to influence. Beware!"*

There has been talk of Hillary Clinton running for president in 2016. I am not specifically saying that she will run for president; although, from what I have seen, it would not surprise me. Regardless, the Father has been clear that the Church must be on guard against her influence and plans to control, whatever way that manifests itself. We must also be aware that Benghazi was a prophetic warning of things to come, that we must pray for light to be shed in the dark places.

5. ISRAEL

The fifth and final area that the Father showed me the body of Christ must change its position on is the nation of Israel. There must be a unification in the American church in support of Israel, including not only prayer but also taking a stand against the Islamic movement in the Middle East. The following is a dream that I had concerning Egypt and Israel:

On the night of November 21, 2012, I had a dream where I was in the country of Egypt and in their capital city of Cairo. I looked up in the sky and saw a gigantic two-headed serpent that stretched as far as my eyes could see.

I was filled with terror and the Spirit of God immediately spoke to me and said, *"Though their speech is as smooth as butter, murder is in their hearts."*

I then saw a man who stood from a balcony of a government building. I recognized that he was a man of great authority as he cried out and said, "Let the nations rejoice! Let Syria rejoice! Let Iran rejoice! Let Libya rejoice!"

The Spirit of God spoke to me again and said, *"Will Egypt not become like Absalom? Will they not wait by Israel's city gates in an attempt to rally the nations together? Are they not acting as an advocate like Absalom was crying out? He said, 'If only I were given more power.' Is the man you saw not crying out, 'If only I was given more power?' Just as Absalom grew weary with his position after four years, watch and see as the nation of Egypt grows weary in the coming years with its position toward Israel."*

The Spirit of God continued and said, *"Israel must not trust the Egyptians. The land of Egypt will become a point of penetration for Muslim nations in the coming years in an attempt to overthrow Jerusalem."*

"Man the walls of Jerusalem," says the Lord. *"You must pray for Netanyahu.*

Cindy Jacobs, you must pray for Netanyahu.

Chuck Pierce, you must pray for Netanyahu.

Mike Bickle, you must pray for Netanyahu.

Lou Engle, you must pray for Netanyahu.

Carlos Sarmiento, you must pray for Netanyahu.

Rick Joyner, you must pray for Netanyahu, for he is my appointed man in this hour. He has my exceedingly great wisdom and understanding into the days that are ahead.

My church must pray that the secrecy in Egypt be exposed. The United States must take its rightful place as the defender and protector of Israel. It is their chosen destiny. Man has chosen Egypt, but I have chosen the United States," says the Lord.

"The only war worth fighting for is a war defending Israel," says the Lord. *"All other wars in the Middle East will be costly and in vain. Do not waste American resources in the Middle East. It is a trap. American weaponry will be used against Israel in the coming years.*

Watch Iraq. Their government is unstable. It will revert back to its old ways and will be a black eye in the face of the United States.

Watch Iran. Treachery is brewing. They will turn on Israel. Syria is a nation of a different kind of evil. Watch the two-headed serpent. Watch in the coming years. See if the nations do not rally to her while she claims to have Israel's best interest in mind. It is a lie!"

As soon as I heard the word "lie" in the dream, I was startled and awakened by the smoke alarms going off in my home. They beeped twice and then not again. I looked at the clock, and it was 2:00 AM. There was no fire in the house. The smoke detector was not broken. There was nothing to be alarmed about. I looked down and realized that I was sweating all over my body. I had just had an incredibly intense dream, and I believe I was awakened by a supernatural occurrence.

SYRIA

Several days later, the Spirit gave me another dream and revisited the word about Syria when He said, *"Syria is a nation of a different kind of evil."*

In this dream, the Holy Spirit began to reveal to me why Syria is a nation of a different kind of evil. He opened up my eyes to see mass genocide and chemical weapons being released upon the people. Bashar Assad has great plans to exterminate many more people than he already has.

The Holy Spirit also revealed to me a terrorist network that is going to come forth out of the nation of Syria that will be new in nature. Among other terrorist networks in the Middle East, this network will be known as a special force unit. It will have ties to many countries in the Middle East.

I also saw a young people's movement coming up out of Syria and even this new terrorist network consisting of many young people. We must keep an eye on these countries and how they might affect the nation of Israel.

MONGOLOID FROM THE SOUTH

After the Father showed me these five areas that were on His heart which He is graciously giving the Church four years to change positions on, I was shown a very strange scene in the dream that I still have a vague understanding of.

As previously stated, over every city in America were the hospitals that had been built over them. The dream began with women in labor, but as the Father spoke over the loud speakers, the cries ceased. Jezebel began to gather her demonic army, and then I was shown the five areas. After this, I was taken to somewhere in the South of the United States. I feel as though I was somewhere around Georgia/Florida. The voice of the Father spoke to me in the dream and said, *"The mongoloid will be birthed from the South."* I then witnessed a woman giving birth to a mangled and distorted looking infant.

I will offer an interpretation from my time seeking the Lord on this, but I admit that I could be wrong. With that being said, I believe that this mongoloid has to do with politics and the 2016 election. This mongoloid has to do with the Republican and Democratic parties possibly being molded together and forming some strange views. I almost sense that it could have something to do with a potential candidate switching sides or one who will arise with a conglomeration of beliefs from each party. Either way, the Father showed me that this mongoloid is going to be birthed from the South and could have ties to Georgia or Florida.

After I saw this woman give birth and heard the Father speak, I woke up from this powerful dream. My prayer is that you would seek the Father on these things that I have shared in this dream and hold onto them for perspective and insight.

Jeremiah Johnson

4

December 15, 2012

SANDY HOOK ELEMENTARY SHOOTINGS

O n the night that tragedy struck our nation in Newton, Connecticut, I prayed before I went to bed that the Spirit of God might give me insight into what He was doing in the school systems and among families. The following is the dream that I had:

I found myself walking the streets of America and witnessing hundreds of thousands of women shouting and screaming. I ran ahead of the crowd to see the banner they were all marching behind. The banner read "Mother's Liberation Movement." For a second, I thought I was in the 1970s among the "Women's Liberation Movement" but realized that I was in 2012 at the "Mother's Liberation Movement."

I admit that I was quite confused in the dream, so I asked the Holy Spirit to explain to me what was happening. This is what He said: *"In the 1970s, a women's liberation movement in America was birthed to set women free from the home and into the workplace. In the days in which you live, a mother's liberation movement is being birthed that will set mothers free from the workplace and back into their homes. While the Women's Liberation Movement sought to empower women away from the home, this mother's movement that I am birthing in America is empowering women back into the home."*

I immediately said to the Spirit, "I don't think this is going to go over well with women." He said to me, *"It's not about the women. It's about their children. Families have become greedy. They have decided to live above their means, and it has driven many mothers back to the workplace, sacrificing precious time with their children. I am liberating them back to the home. Watch and see."*

At this point in the dream, I began to visit hundreds of elementary schools all over America. When I arrived at each school, I could not get in the door because there was a long line of women standing out front. I decided to wait in the line but never asked what was happening. I got to the front desk and was met by a very upset woman. She said to me, "Are you withdrawing your child from school too?" I said, "I don't have a child in school, but is this what the future holds?" She said to me, "Mothers from all over the nation are withdrawing their children from school and are now schooling them at home. They have told us that since we have taken God out of school, they are taking their children out of school."

I was stunned and walked out of the elementary school unable to believe what I had just heard. The final stop I made in the dream was to various neighborhoods in America. I knocked on doors in neighborhoods to see if what the woman at the school had said was true. Much to my amazement, it was! I walked into many houses with worship music playing and mothers educating their children. The atmosphere was filled with so much joy and delight. In the last house I visited, the woman who answered the door asked me if I would like to see her basement. She opened the door and let me walk down the stairs.

I looked around and noticed an inscription in the foundation of this house. When I saw it, I immediately knew it was from the Father. It read, *"I am restoring the family in this hour, but you must know that this word will be rejected by many. The continued violence in the school systems will be a sign to many that they must begin to teach their children in the home."*

I walked back up the stairs and was met by the woman who let me in her home. She said to me, "Do you know who I am?" I said, "No, ma'am, I don't." She said, "I once was a teacher like so many, but the Holy Spirit convicted me in such a powerful way to begin to teach in my home. As I followed His leading, many other teachers like myself began to withdraw and form communities all over America where we now teach our children in loving, Christian environments. Even our local churches are coming under the conviction of the Holy Spirit. You would not believe how many preschools, day care centers, and Christian schools are being birthed out of churches all over America because of the violence in the school systems. The Mother's Liberation Movement in America has saved so many lives."

Then I awoke.

5

January 4, 2013

THE BLACK PLAGUE COMING TO THE SCHOOL SYSTEMS

I continue to have very disturbing dreams about the violence coming to the school systems in America. In my dream, I witnessed a black wave which was a plague sweeping through the nation and overtaking the youth of our day. It was the spirit of death and suicide. There began to be town hall meetings all over the United States as parents began to literally tremble at the strength of the black plague.

While the parents became angry and upset at the government and school system, the spirit of prophecy overtook me. At a large gathering of these parents I said, *"'Shall you blame the government for the lack of attention your children suffer from? Has the government bought your children Christmas toys that fascinate them with things of the world? I rebuke you parents of America for caring more about your career and your life than your children,'* says the Lord. *'The price that many are going to pay will be unbearable. Yes, the weeping and wailing in America over the spirit of suicide, causing many murders in the school system, will be the price that too many pay for ignoring their children. As the spirit of suicide controls a youth, Satan will convince that youth to murder other youths. The education system has become Satan's playground because of the failure of the family unit in America,'* says the Lord."

He continued, *"'Do not be so foolish as to blame the government and school system for the lack of safety for your children, for you have not been faithful to provide safety for their hearts and minds within your homes. You must repent. You must shift your attention at home in order to stop the black plague.'"*

6

January 24, 2013

SHOTS FIRED AT THE WHITE HOUSE

In the dream, I found myself in Washington D.C. right outside the White House. In a matter of moments, there was a tremendous voice that boomed and said,

"SHOTS FIRED, SHOTS FIRED, SHOTS FIRED, SHOTS FIRED."

My instant reaction was to run because the crowd went into total chaos and confusion, but my feet wouldn't move. Fear was literally controlling thousands of people as they ran, but something unusual caught my eye. I began to stare into some of the eyes of those that were running, and they revealed themselves to me as demons.

I instantly realized that all those fleeing right outside the White House, as the voice yelled *"SHOTS FIRED,"* were not only demons but people controlled and given over to the sinful nature. The voice that was yelling "*SHOTS FIRED*" was actually causing the demonic voices and people walking in evil to flee.

As the streets cleared, I saw twelve people bowing down side-by-side facing the White House with their faces to the ground; they were worshipping Jesus. Suddenly, I noticed an angelic army above me carrying weapons of warfare, but the angels had looks of great anguish upon their faces.

Tears filled my eyes as I recognized that these angels were longing to hear the prayers of the saints. It was as if they could not be released to assist the saints until "shots were fired" that would send them on assignment.

What I thought began in the dream as "shots fired" and innocent civilians running for their lives because of evil, actually became a dream about prayers that need to be lifted - and are going to be lifted - outside of the White House to assign an angelic army with weapons of warfare to the body of Christ. If we do not pray, they will not be released to assist and aid us in our fight against evil in America.

As the twelve people outside the White House continued to worship Jesus and pray, the angelic army, upon hearing the prayers, began to be released to the praying church. There was one angel, the angel Gabriel, with a sword in his hand that was leading all of the other angels as he wore a breastplate that read, "The manifold wisdom of God is being made known through the Church to the rulers and the authorities in the heavenly realms."

Then I awoke.

I prophesy that the White House is going to become a place where intercessors and leaders everywhere gather to call upon the name of Jesus and release an angelic army to assist the end time Church. We must recognize that unless we pray, the manifold wisdom of God cannot be released to them. It is through our mouths that the plans of the Lord will reach not only the angels but those who need the gospel.

Stand with me and believe that an army will one day stand before the White House and declare, *"SHOTS FIRED, SHOTS FIRED, SHOTS FIRED!"*

7

February 21, 2013

A GENERATION OF JOBS AND JOSEPHS

I was shown a generation of "Jobs" and "Josephs" who are being groomed in America in these days. They are/have experienced great trial, loss, and pain. But behold! They will arise in America after 2016 when President Obama leaves office.

These "Jobs" and "Josephs" will be people of influence and prosperity. They will one day bring great reformation to this nation but must submit to the process. America is going through a four year economic drought that will come to an end in 2016. God showed me that He is refusing and will refuse to bless the work of President Obama's hands.

I asked the Father how His people will survive through these next four years of economic drought. He said, *"Jeremiah, I am releasing a revelation of My sovereignty that will serve as the life source of my people. What will keep my "Jobs" and "Josephs" alive during the next four years is a revelation of My sovereignty, and it will be what gives them incredible success after 2016."*

He said one last thing: *"Tell the people in America that I am so secure in My sovereignty that I'm not in the least bit afraid of things looking like I'm not sovereign."*

8

March 20, 2013

THE HEART OF THE FATHER

I found myself as a guest speaker at a large prophetic conference. No one knew who I was, and I was the youngest speaker there by twenty years. There was some incredible worship going on, and then I was to lead the afternoon session. As I worshipped, I prayed to the Father for some words for people, but nothing came. I felt nervous because this is unusual for me.

After worship, I took the stage and asked everyone to stand. I thought that I would start off by prophesying to some folks. As I made my way to the first man, I opened up my mouth, but what came totally shocked me - sobbing! I went to the next person and opened up my mouth - no words again - just sobbing. This happened over and over again. Then I went and placed my hands on a woman who had back problems. As I went to "speak to the back problems," all

I did was sob over her. As I cried my eyes out over her, she suddenly became angry saying, "That's enough!"

I walked to the front of the conference and said to the Father, "What is happening? I have no words for these people, just sobs." He said to me, *"I have called you to share and impart My heart through tears. Stop focusing on the words. I've called you to share the Father's heart."* He continued on, *"I am deeply troubled and grieved with the prophetic movement in the earth. From my perspective, there are only two types of prophetic gatherings. There are gatherings where people only want My words, and there are gatherings where people want My heart. Chasing after My words leads to spiritual immaturity. Pursuing My heart leads to maturity and eternal life."*

As I shared this with those present, half of them got up and walked out, including the lady I had prayed for with back pain. I called out to her from the stage, "It's not His words that would have healed you, but His heart!" Then I prophesied to the crowd of those who remained, "Beware of those that carry the Word of God without the heart of the Father. If we know His heart, we will know what He knows. Many gathered around the Son to hear His words but had no interest in connecting with the heart of the Father. They were blind. The primary purpose of the Son coming to the earth was the introduction and revelation of the heart of the Father."

9

April 6, 2013

VISITATION FROM JESUS CHRIST: BAPTISM OF DISCIPLINE

I n this dream, the Lord Jesus Christ was standing in front of me wearing a white robe, and there was fire in His eyes. A man was standing to my left, and Jesus pointed at him and said, *"I have created you for the ministry. Why are you not doing what I asked you to do?"*

As this question was asked, this man began to tremble, and so did I. The Lord extended His arms towards us as a wave of scorching fire swept over us. That is the only way that I know to describe what happened. I do not believe the Lord Jesus was angry, but there was a weightiness and sobriety upon His face and actions.

As the wave of scorching fire hit myself and this man, I sat up in my bed in the middle of the night soaked in sweat and looked at my alarm clock. It was 3:33 AM.

As I sat in silence catching my breath, I heard the voice of the Father. He said to me, *"I am going to baptize this generation with the fire of My discipline and chastisement because I love them and because they refuse to do what I have asked them to do."*

This is a call to a slumbering generation of leaders. The man in my dream represents a generation of leaders that the Father has called into the ministry who are not doing what He has asked them to do. There is an urgency for them to awaken to their destiny and call.

The Father continued to speak to me and said, *"I do not make eternal investments in the lives of My people to watch them grow lazy and apathetic."*

I began to weep as the Father told me this, and I said to Him, "What has this generation done to warrant chastisement and discipline because this is not the primary way that You deal with us as Your children?"

The Holy Spirit immediately reminded me of 1 Cor 11:31-32, in the context of the Lord's supper where it says, "We would not have been disciplined so severely if we would have judged ourselves in the right manner."

The Father is releasing a baptism of fire through chastisement and discipline because of the failure to judge ourselves in the right manner. It is better that we judge ourselves than when He judges us.

We must head the call to holiness, righteousness, and pure living. The Father is after awakening and dealing with leaders in whom He has made an eternal investment to see His purposes fulfilled in the earth.

10

April 17, 2013

THE PROPHET'S BREAD

I had an incredible dream in which the Spirit showed me a select group of people in the earth who are crying out asking, "Where is the prophet's bread?" These people are frustrated and confused at times because they continue to deliver the true word of the Lord while their families starve, but other people who occupy high positions in the church are wealthy and have compromised the message. The Spirit spoke to me in the midst of their cries and gave me directions for these prophetic people who are being faithful to declare the word of the Lord regardless of the response and are struggling financially. He said to tell them three things:

1. "Make up your mind. Are you going to serve Me or serve man?"

2. He is releasing the "ravens of America" in this hour. It was

incredible what I saw, but there are people in the U.S. that are actually going to finance prophets, not the Church. He is raising up people that will sow into the unadulterated and pure word of the Lord, and they will be incredibly blessed by it. Prophets will minister in the Church, but the "ravens" will feel specifically burdened to sow into the rhema of God.

3 "You must find your identity in Me. Beware of thinking that because people have rejected you, I have rejected you. It's not the truth."

11

April 25, 2013

LIFE DREAM FOR CENTRAL FLORIDA

In my dream, I was shown a map of Central Florida, and the word "life" was written on it. I then saw huge gatherings of Hispanic people in Central Florida, and they were crying out saying, "Give us the torch."

Then the Spirit of God spoke to me in the dream and said, *"Central Florida is the forerunner for the Life Movement in the earth. I am giving the torch to the Hispanic populations. They must run with this message."*

The next thing I saw was a curse that has settled upon Central Florida since 2008. For seven years demonic activity has attempted to abort the dreams and visions of God. It will end in 2015. Fire will fall in 2016. The Spirit said to me, *"Jeremiah, there is very little power and authority in the dream and life realms in Central Florida, but, behold, you will see breakthrough. Many of My servants have been sidelined. This seven year period has nearly cost them everything, but My purposes will be fulfilled. Run after adoption. Run after it hard, but do not use it as an excuse not to make a stand publicly."*

12

April 27, 2013

THE DECEIVED CHURCH DREAM

As I was sleeping the Spirit of God said to me, *"Jeremiah, I want to show you how Satan is deceiving the body of Christ."* I said, "Okay, Lord, show me." To my great surprise He took me to several evangelistic outreach events. Many believers had gathered there in an attempt to win the lost and save souls. There was excitement in the air, but I noticed something strange. The believers who had gathered had no family there with them.

At that moment, a great wind began to blow and darkness covered the sky. All the believers began to cry out that the storm might pass so that they could continue evangelizing and reaching out. Suddenly, the voice of God spoke like lightning. *"I sent this storm! You are deceived!"* I will never forget the looks on people's faces.

He continued, *"You are reaching out to families, but I ask you, where is your family? You go to the mission field. What about your family? You seek to rescue men and women in distress. Is your marriage not in distress? You have a heart for orphans. Are your own children not orphans because of the time you spend away from them doing ministry and evangelizing? GO HOME!"*

As everyone exited the big field where they had been evangelizing, I remained there with the Father. It began to rain, and He said to me, *"Jeremiah, I want you to feel my tears."* I stood there in the rain for several minutes, but this rain was like no rain I had ever felt before. This rain was the tears of the Father for His children. He said to me, *"Jeremiah, so many tears! So many tears come before me. The tears are from the wives and children of pastors and leaders who have been deceived by Satan himself into thinking that lost souls are more important than the souls of their own family. Satan is opening up deceptive ministry doors in this hour in an attempt to divert the body of Christ away from healthy marriages and strong families."*

I said, "I'm not sure what to say Father." He replied, *"If you only knew, Son. If you only knew how many sons and daughters hate Me because their parent who claimed to serve Me was never home. Their parent who claimed to serve Me would rather serve orphans than their own children. The call of so many future leaders has been aborted by none other than those future leaders' parents. They were terrible examples to their children of what really matters in the Kingdom."*

13

May 1, 2013

TERRORIST NETWORK COMING TO THE UNITED STATES

In my dream I was following a terrorist network that had come to the United States to specifically, as they said, "Obstruct religious freedom in America." I was trying to warn people that they were going to bomb a major city in the United States, but everyone was too busy and would not listen to me.

When the bomb exploded in a major city, I ran to that city and sat upon a hill to watch the chaos. As I waited on the hill, pastors and leaders began to come up to me and ask me to speak in their churches. I went to a special meeting with leaders in the city where the blast took place, and they were speaking of revival. They began to demand that I perform miraculous signs and wonders so that the city would turn to the Lord. Filled with frustration, I stood up and began to rebuke them. I told them that what America needs is not signs and wonders but to repent for their wickedness. The leaders and pastors were so surprised. I then quoted them Matt 11 and told them that this attack that they had witnessed in America is just the beginning of terrorist networks working within the United States to "obstruct religious freedom."

Then I awoke.

14

May 7, 2013

THE EAGLE HAS LANDED

I found myself in a very unusual airport. The first thing I noticed was that there was only one plane taking off. The second thing I recognized was that all the flights that were coming in were flights where people did not have their luggage because of missed connections. The airport was in total chaos as everyone was terrified to get on the one plane that was taking off. No one had their luggage, and it was the day before Christmas.

I started looking closely at all the people frantically searching for their luggage as a last call to get on the one plane was issued. Suddenly, I noticed something that changed everything! As I strained my eyes to look at the screens where people were watching, I read this:

"Baggage from Philadelphia: cell 1."

"Baggage from New York: cell 2."

As I read the words on the screen, I began yelling and said, "This is not your luggage! It's your baggage! It's a trap. You must leave your baggage and run quickly because the Eagle has landed and will most certainly leave you behind if you do not act now. You must run for the Eagle. Your luggage is on the Eagle. It's called your identity!"

Some people recognized what I had said and began to run for the Eagle whose engines were already running. I ran over to a crowd gathered around a large cell called "Baggage from Atlanta: cell 3" and told them what was happening, but no one was moving. I fought my way to the middle of the crowd but was stunned when I saw a black man in a three piece suit preaching to people with a pulpit and Bible. He said, "Welcome to my church where I will teach you how to manage your baggage." The crowd cheered, but I began to weep. I cried out and said, "The great deception in America has begun. He who has ears to hear let him listen to what I am about to say. False teachers and preachers are being elevated in the body of Christ at an alarming rate. They are deceiving people with their sin management messages, which they call "grace," and blinding people from the truth. You must leave your baggage behind in order to enter the Kingdom of Heaven. The Eagle has landed and is now taking off. Repent and receive your new identity or be deceived by false teachers and preachers."

Someone asked me, "Where are the false teachers and preachers coming from?" I answered, "Atlanta, GA; Tampa, FL; Houston, TX; Los Angeles, California; and Colorado Springs, Colorado."

Then I awoke.

15

May 30, 2013

HELL IS FOR REAL

In this dream, I found myself walking in a structure like a dungeon where all I could hear was weeping and gnashing of teeth. There was a feeling of surprise in this room, almost like gasps of "I can't believe I'm here" from those I could hear moaning and crying.

I walked up to a large door that was closed, and on the door was an inscription that read, *"THOSE WHO PRACTICE SUCH THINGS WILL NOT INHERIT THE KINGDOM OF HEAVEN."*

The door opened up into a large gym, and as I began to walk around, there were fifteen stations set up for the people who were present. The atmosphere was very intense, and no one seemed to notice me. After a while, I realized that these people were incapable of doing anything other than staying at these stations as if they were slaves.

The Holy Spirit began to speak to me as I walked around and asked me if I knew the "love wins" doctrine. "Yes," I replied, and He continued on saying, *"Do you see all of this? This is why love does not win. This is why justice wins."*

Then I awoke.

EXPLANATION

As I sat up in my bed, I immediately recognized the phrase written on the door in hell that led me to that room resembling a gym. It was from Gal 5:21, "…as I have forewarned you that those who practice such things shall not inherit the Kingdom of God."

I recalled from the dream that there were fifteen stations where people were working. As soon as I recognized this, I got my uncle on the phone, a man well studied in the Greek language, and had him read this section from the original Greek text. I asked him how many "works of the flesh" are mentioned in Gal 5:19-21, and discovered, just as I suspected, that there are exactly fifteen "works of the flesh" mentioned in this passage.

I believe that I visited a place in hell where those who practice the "works of the flesh" listed in Gal 5:19-21 will be sent.

Upon even further study in the Greek language, I found that the word "practice" actually means, "to exercise or to carry on one's affairs." This would explain why I entered into a gym-like setting. I do not believe that those who at times - or rarely - choose to engage in the "works of the flesh" are going to hell. I believe I was being shown that those who exercise and carry on the affairs of the "works of the flesh" upon the earth will be sent to hell. It speaks of a lifestyle, a life committed or busy with the "works of the flesh" that will reap eternal torment.

.

16

June 20, 2013

THE DAYS OF KING HEZEKIAH: A WARNING ABOUT PRESIDENT OBAMA

I found myself pulling up carpet for a living. As I would enter large buildings to tear up the old carpet, I began to cry out hysterically to anyone who would listen, "We are living in the days of King Hezekiah!" I would shout this phrase over and over again to puzzled onlookers, whom I realized thought I was a raving lunatic. I pulled up to my last job in my carpet truck and saw that it was the White House in Washington D.C.

I walked inside and began tearing up the carpet and yelling, "We are living in the days of King Hezekiah!" The White House staff became alarmed and gathered around me as I began to weep. As I was crawling around on my hands and knees weeping uncontrollably, this is what I told them:

"Is it not written in the book you workers of iniquity? Was it not in the days of King Hezekiah where he foolishly welcomed the Babylonians into his kingdom, and there was nothing in his house nor in all his dominion that Hezekiah did not show the Babylonians? Behold, President Obama has acted foolishly. He has welcomed the Muslim Brotherhood into the White House. He has welcomed assassins who have been trained to kill the patriotic spirit. President Obama has formed an unholy alliance with Hillary Clinton. They wish to welcome the Islamic regime into America. He is and will continue to appoint strategic men and women in positions of authority to pave the way for Hillary."

At this point in the dream, the White House staff had attacked me and thrown me out on the White House steps.

I got into my carpet truck and drove to a meeting of church leaders who were anxiously awaiting my arrival. Everyone seemed to know that I had entered the White House and prophesied to the staff. I walked into the meeting with the pastors and leaders and gave them a message. This is what the Lord says:

"The end time church must not be deceived in this hour. They must intercede that the Muslim Brotherhood be exposed. Beware of the contact that Mohammed Morsi and President Obama have. America must not make a pact with Egypt against Israel. The will on Capitol Hill is demonically influenced. Even now I am breathing upon Rubio. Even now I am breathing upon those who carry the patriotic spirit of America. This nation must return to Me with weeping and wailing. They must

pray for deception and demonic strategy to be revealed among President Obama and Hillary Clinton."

I walked off the stage, and then I awoke.

17

June 25, 2013

RENT A MINISTRY

In this dream, I was driving down a highway and noticed a large car dealership on my left that displayed very flashy and expensive cars. As I passed the dealership, my eyes were drawn to a large sign in the parking lot that read "Rent a Ministry."

After reading the sign, I slammed on my brakes and pulled into the parking lot because I wanted to know what the sign meant. As I got out of my car to go inside, I noticed the line to get into the dealership was significantly long. Many people in line had flashy pieces of paper in hand, so I walked up to one man and asked what he was holding. He replied, "These are my ministry credentials." Everyone in the line nodded their heads in agreement and showed me that they had theirs too.

I decided that I did not want to wait in line but wanted to find a way inside the dealership. To my surprise, I walked to the front, and the security team led me to the showroom floor.

Suddenly, I found myself surrounded by exotic cars and very excited people in line. Everyone was running up to these extravagant cars, falling in love with them, then taking their ministry credentials and slapping them on the backs of the cars where the license plates should be.

There was a showroom full of these overly excited people in fancy cars with their ministry credentials slapped on the backs of their vehicles. All at once, everyone was shouting for the keys so they could start their cars. Out of the back came a sad old man with tears in his eyes. On one arm were all the keys to the cars. He was wearing tattered clothes, and when he turned around everyone in the dealership gasped. He had fresh stripes on his back and was bleeding.

All the drivers in the dealership now stared at this man as he began to weep uncontrollably. He got down on both of his knees and cried out to the drivers, "For who makes you different from anyone else? What do you have that you did not receive? And if you did receive it, why do you boast as though you did not? Already you have all you want! Already you have become rich! You have begun to reign—and that without us! How I wish that you really had begun to reign so that we also might reign with you! For it seems to me that God has put us apostles on display at the end of the procession, like those condemned to die in the arena. We have been made a spectacle to the whole universe, to angels as well as to human beings. We are fools for Christ, but you are so wise in Christ! We are weak, but you are strong! You are honored. We are dishonored! To this very hour we go hungry and thirsty. We are in rags. We are treated brutally. We are homeless. We work hard with our own hands. When we are cursed, we bless; when we are persecuted, we endure it; when we are slandered, we answer kindly. We have become the scum of the earth, the garbage of the world— right up to this moment."

As the weeping old man with bleeding scars on his back said this, the people in the fancy cars with their ministry credentials as their license plates began to say to one another, "I have never heard of that rhetoric before. This old man is insane."

As I listened on the showroom floor to the people in the cars, I began to weep and shout, "You fools! Is this man not from the former generation and quoting 1 Cor 4, which you seem not to know? You think that your credentials and desires to rent ministries, though they cost you nothing, are pleasing in the sight of God? Behold, I pronounce to you the curse on this current generation which is the spirit of entitlement. It has come like a plague and is robbing the saints of heavenly rewards. I tell you, storehouses in heaven are empty, Beloved. Men and women have desired their rewards upon the earth and stored nothing in heaven! There must be a shift. Blind eyes must be opened. Ministers must be taught the price that they must pay for the sake of His name. What will it benefit you to have human credentials but none with God? This is a time of repentance! Yes, repent and be cleansed every one of you."

Then I awoke.

18

September 15, 2013

A WARNING TO THE SIGNS AND WONDERS MOVEMENT

I walked into a large building where a conference was being held. As I headed towards the registration desk, I was startled to see that the woman checking people in for the conference had a face that appeared to be distorted. I began to look around me, and everyone in the line had distorted bodies and faces.

As I signed in for the conference and walked into the auditorium, there was an unusual sense of excitement in the air. I sat in my seat and was deeply alarmed at all of these people with distorted faces and bodies waiting for the conference speaker to come on the stage.

Suddenly, words came on the screen before the speaker came out. They read, "Welcome to the H. I. A. conference."

The "H" was by itself, but the "I" stood for "impartation," and the "A" stood for "activation." The meaning of "H" was not found on the screen.

No one in the crowd seemed to notice or mind that the letter "H" had no meaning, but I began to get physically ill in my seat until a wave of deep sickness swept over me.

At this point in the dream, Bill Johnson and Randy Clark came out on stage, and the crowd of people with distorted faces and bodies went wild. Many of them began to beat their chests and actually bow down to these men.

When Randy and Bill saw what was happening, they began frantically trying to get this crowd of people not to worship them, but they could not persuade them differently.

I rose to my feet from my seat in the middle of the crowd and began to cry out in a loud voice, "It is not impartation and activation that you need but deep inner healing of your soul. The 'H' stands for 'inner healing.' Do not be deceived! Getting hands laid on you and moving in spiritual gifts will not save you on judgment day. Why has this movement forsaken the cross? Why are you worshipping mere men?"

The crowd became silent, and every one of them put their heads down in shame. By this time, Bill and Randy were sobbing on the stage. They were crying saying, "Is this what we dreamed of? Is this what the movement has come to? Here we stand before a generation of people hungry for impartation and activation but who know nothing of inner healing that leads to the cross."

As Bill and Randy wept and finished speaking, I cried out again and said, "Behold! The Father is calling this movement back to the nursery. Yes, you must be rocked like babies and have the 'Song of the Redeemed' sung over you. Every one of you, follow me!"

I left where I was standing and took this entire conference crowd into a nursery that was as big as a football field. In the nursery were thousands of rocking chairs, each ready for one of these people with distorted faces and bodies to be rocked and sung over.

Each person found a chair and looked at me and said, "Who will rock us and heal our wounds, and what is the 'Song of the Redeemed?'"

I looked at them and said, "The Father will rock you, Jesus will heal your wounds, and the 'Song of the Redeemed' that will be played over you is called 'Open Wide' by Suzy Willis Yaraei." Everyone climbed into their rocking chair, and the music began.

"Getting us ready you are
Touching places still dark
Deep inside of us
King of glory come in

Messing us up you are
Setting us up for
Eternal love oh
King of glory come in

Open wide
Open wide and we will usher you in
Open wide
Open wide oh king of glory come in

We're not holding on anymore
To the keys to the doors
We give them to you
King of glory come in

Oil the hinges on the gates
Turn the lock, roll the stones away
We call to you, oh King of glory come in"

After the "Song of the Redeemed" ended, I awoke.

19

October 15, 2013

A WARNING TO PROPHETS AND THE PROPHETIC MOVEMENT

I had a dream where the Spirit of God revealed to me that Satan is inciting the prophets of God to prophesy from the place of anger, rather than from the place of peace that can only come from the Spirit of God. This is a direct attempt to discredit the ministry of the prophet in the earth.

I found myself walking through a forest with thousands of prophets, and as we came to an opening in the forest, a large lake appeared in front of us. Now, the journey through the forest had taken many days, and a number of the prophets were exhausted and dying of thirst.

As the prophets saw the lake appear before them, many went into a full sprint without looking into the water. I found it interesting that many of those running to the water were older, seasoned prophets that I recognized. As I watched them run, I suddenly looked at the water in the lake, and to my horror, it was polluted and contaminated with all sorts of waste and trash.

As the prophets drank, I looked around me and realized that there were only a few of us who recognized that though we were very thirsty from our journey, the polluted and contaminated water was not healthy and was not from the Spirit.

I began to weep in the dream and said to the Father, "What is wrong with these prophets? Are they blind? They have become like Esau who out of his exhaustion traded his birth right for a bowl of soup."

The Father responded back to me in the dream and said, *"Jeremiah, many prophets in America are drinking polluted and contaminated waters because they are tired and weary. They are giving in to anger and bitterness toward President Obama and the United States. They are prophesying out of the flesh and exchanging the pure word of My Spirit for meaningless chatter that stirs up the people. They are mere false alarms."*

I fell on my knees in the dream and said, "Have you heard all these words from the prophets, Father? They are prophesying of military takeover, the Russians coming, martial law, natural disasters, and more. Who am I, a young boy, to warn all these seasoned prophets of the waters of Marah? They will not listen to me!"

The Father spoke to me again and said, *"Do not tell Me what they will and will not do. You prophesy to the prophetic movement, and you warn them of the enemy inciting them to prophesy from the place of anger. My prophets must learn how to separate patriotism from what I am saying and doing. My prophets must learn how to separate their fears and worries from what I am saying and doing."*

As the Father said this, I immediately woke up from this dream and sat up in my bed. The Holy Spirit immediately gave me Deut 29:29 which says, "The secret things belong to the Lord our God, but the things revealed belong to us and to our sons forever, that we may observe all the words of this law."

I said to the Holy Spirit, "What are you trying to tell me through this verse?"

He said, *"You prophets believe that maturity looks like having a word for every event. I say maturity looks like not having to have a word for every event, unless I give you one. Do you not know that many prophets in the earth are simply prophesying from the flesh because they are upset that I have not said anything to them concerning the state of America? It is merely their pride and desire to be seen and heard that causes them to operate in anger and prophesy. Let it not be so with you!"*

I am asking as someone within the prophetic movement, that you consider this dream and what the Father has spoken to me. I recognize that we all see in part and have a different piece of the puzzle. I believe, with all of my heart, that the enemy wants the prophets of God to drink from the waters of Marah. Satan wants to incite the prophets to prophesy from the place of anger which will lead to misdirection, false prophecy, fear, panic, and more.

I am **NOT** at all saying that words of warning and impending destruction are not from God. What I am saying is that many prophetic words coming forth are being delivered from the place of anger. Prophets are being invited out of their weariness and tiredness to drink polluted and contaminated waters that are not from the Spirit of God.

We need to pray for real wisdom in this hour. We as prophetic people need to check our filters and ask the Holy Spirit to remove any unrighteous anger and bitterness in our hearts toward President Obama and America that will cause us to prophesy misdirected, false words to the people. May the Father grant us a needed spirit of wisdom and revelation within the prophetic movement.

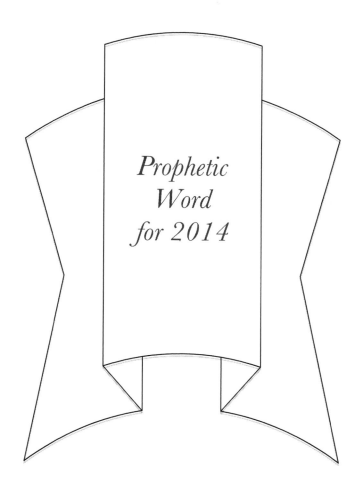

Prophetic Word for 2014

20

PREPARATION IN THE MIDST OF UNCERTAINTY

As I have sat before the counsel of the Lord and sought wisdom, insight, and understanding into the year 2014, it has become increasingly apparent to me that the Father is not only desiring to share with us specifically what to watch for, but more importantly, how we can and must prepare for the days ahead.

The Word of God is filled with predictions and prophecies that fall into two categories. The first category is the "I Wills" of God. These words were ones that would surely come to pass and gave no opportunity for the people of God to repent so that the impending "I will" could be avoided or met with less severity. (Jer 15:1-2)

The second category is the "If You Wills" of God. These words were dependent upon the response of the hearer. Take for example Jonah and the city of Nineveh. Judgment and destruction were prophesied by Jonah, but because of deep repentance over sin and the response of the people, judgment and destruction were avoided. (Jonah 3:1-10)

It is very important that we understand as believers what category the word of the Lord falls into so that we can pray and prepare accordingly. If an "I Will" of the Lord has been released and nothing can be done to prevent it, we need to begin to cry out for severe mercy and submit to the plans of the Father, rather than act and pray ignorantly of His will.

If the word of the Lord is conditional and is an "If You Will" prediction and prophecy, the body of Christ needs to respond in intercession, humility, and with fasting. If the Father sees the response that He is looking for, then we do have the power to partner with His purposes. It is not that we are changing the mind of God in these circumstances, but that we are responding to His warnings in a way that pleases Him and causes Him to relent.

I sense very strongly that the following prophecies and predictions for the year 2014 are conditional. They are "If You Will" words. I believe that the body of Christ can and will play a major role in determining the impact of these coming events. I want to reiterate one more time: The Father is not only desiring to alert us to what is coming in the days ahead, but more importantly, He wants to show us how to prepare for the days ahead! The future in these matters is uncertain because it is largely based upon how we choose to prepare and respond to the word of the Lord.

I want to prophesy that the call for humility and the need to fast and pray in 2014 will become more apparent and clear than ever before. Families, churches, ministries, businesses, and the political world are going to see with ever increasing clarity the need for supernatural intervention in 2014. The words: **stronghold, gridlock,** and **stalemate** are going to become catch phrases in 2014. These terms will be used to describe many world events as well as personal, ministry-related, and business circumstances. The Holy Spirit reassured me that through humility, prayer, and fasting we will see breakthrough, victory, and advancement.

In other words, the year of 2014 will be one in which the body of Christ walks in humility, prayer, and fasting. These three pillars are weapons in the hands of the saints that will bring breakthrough, victory, and advancement as strongholds, gridlocks, and stalemates present themselves before us. Marriages are going to depend on this strategy in 2014.

All-night prayer gatherings, corporate and family fasts, prophetic words, and messages from behind the pulpit will begin to target the need to walk humbly before man and our God. Even some politicians will begin to call for prayer and fasting in 2014 as they recognize the need for the hand and wisdom of God in their midst.

Four Prophetic Words for the Year 2014:

1. The Rise and Fall of Ministers

The Holy Spirit has continually taken me to 1 Cor 3:1-11 as I have prayed about 2014. Specifically, verses 3 and 4 and verse 11 have become so alive in my spirit. Verses 3 and 4 say, "…for you are still fleshly. For since there is jealousy and strife among you, are you not still fleshly, and are you not walking like mere men? For when one says, 'I am of Paul' and another, 'I am of Apollos' are you not mere men?" Verse 11 says, "For no man can lay a foundation other than the one which is laid, which is Jesus Christ."

The year 2014 in the body of Christ will be one of exposure and separation of ministries and churches that are built upon the foundation of the flesh and ministries and churches that are built upon the foundation of Jesus Christ.

Among the men and women that continue to build ministries around themselves, we will witness an exposing of sin and pride like never before. Atlanta, Texas, Florida, and North Carolina are going to see immorality exposed among ministers while poor stewardship of finances will be brought to the light.

In the midst of this turmoil in the body of Christ in 2014, where unhealthy allegiance and soul ties have been formed between ministers and people, the Father is raising up ministers of purity who walk in complete devotion and reliance upon Him. These humble servants of God choose to preach nothing but Christ and Him crucified. These individuals will be a great measure of healing and relief to many who have given up on the body of Christ.

How can we prepare for the rise and fall of ministers in 2014?

We need to pray that ministers will humble themselves and direct people to fix their eyes on Jesus. We need to pray that unhealthy attachment and allegiance to ministers will be exposed and broken in Jesus' name. There is a co-dependency upon man that the Father wants to uncover in 2014 in the body of Christ. If we will pray, I believe the Father will intervene and not only reveal to people where their hope and trust have been placed but also will awaken ministers and save them from operating in the flesh.

2. Increasingly Disoriented Weather Patterns

On October 2nd, I had a dream in which the Spirit of God said to me, *"Beware of increasingly disoriented weather patterns that will seek to destroy the livestock and crop industries."* I published this dream online and within one week, an unusual winter storm hit South Dakota and killed between ten and twenty thousand cattle in one day.

I believe that this is a sign of events to come in 2014. In 2014 we are going to witness very unusual and disoriented weather patterns that will bring destruction not only to livestock and crops but also to the lives of people. The body of Christ needs to be in prayer about the winter season of 2014 and the impact it will have in America. We must be on alert as flooding is another area that the Spirit revealed to me could be potentially destructive.

How can we prepare for increasingly disoriented weather patterns in 2014?

The Holy Spirit spoke to me that we must steward the wealth that He is releasing in the earth. Currently, the reason why the Father is financially blessing many people in America is so that they can come to the aid and rescue of those impacted by these strange weather patterns in 2014. I saw many people opening up benevolence accounts to be used to help finance those in need who will be affected by storms in 2014. The last thing the Holy Spirit showed me in preparing for what is coming is to make sure that you are living in the geographical location He has called you to.

3. Washington D.C. on High Alert

The months of August, September, October, and November in 2014 are going to see a political fiasco in Washington D.C. These months will be a turbulent time in the earth and will involve both financial and military decisions that will impact many. I heard the Spirit of God say that during these months in Washington D.C. that *what is hidden will be revealed.*" We need to be targeting these four months with prayer as it provides a window of opportunity for lies to be exposed and darkness to be brought into the light. There will be a collision between the states in these months, and we must pray for unity in the United States.

How can we prepare for Washington D.C. to go on High Alert in 2014?

We need to pray for our president and our senators. I received a vision of many in the political realm jockeying for position in 2014 that will cause a significant shift in future elections. Pray for darkness and lies to be exposed specifically from August to November and for truth to be shared.

4. China- The Sleeping Giant Will Awake

We are going to see lots of attention and focus on the nation of China in 2014. The Spirit of God began to show me an enormous desire in the government of China to take their place in the earth as a military and economic powerhouse. Look for China to express their disappointment in being disregarded in 2014, but there will be a surge and plans to be recognized as a nation of formidable power. We cannot underestimate this nation's influence in 2014. I heard the Spirit say that, *"What takes place in China in 2014 will touch the four corners of the earth."*

How can we prepare for China- the sleeping giant that will awaken in 2014?

We must pray for the relationship between China and the United States not to become strained. At different times in 2014, as the world shifts its attention to China, pray for wisdom and clarity for world leaders on how to respond to the movement in this country.

The year 2014 will be filled with much uncertainty but will also prove to be a season of great preparation for those seeking to position themselves to be used by God. The outcome and impact of many world events will be dependent upon the response and prayers of the body of Christ. Look for many voices and trumpets to be heard in America and other countries of the earth calling for humility, prayer, and fasting. These three pillars and keys will be mighty weapons in the hand of the Lord in tearing down strongholds and freeing the saints of God to operate as the Spirit leads.

Watch for the rise and fall of ministers in 2014. Look for increasingly disoriented weather patterns in the earth. Keep your eye on Washington D.C., especially during the months of August, September, October, and November. China will seek to position itself in prominent ways in 2014 like never seen before. What happens in that nation in the coming year will impact the four corners of the earth.

*Dreams for
the Days
Ahead*

21

THE RISE OF OBADIAH'S PROPHETS

In September of this year, I received a series of dreams about the shift that the Holy Spirit is bringing to the prophetic movement. In the first dream, the Holy Spirit said to me, *"The days of the 'showdown' prophets are coming to an end. I am raising up a company of prophets that will give their lives to the 'lowdown.'"*

I said to the Holy Spirit in the dream, "I do not understand what you are talking about. Show me this in the Scriptures."

Immediately my very own Bible was placed in front of me and was open to 1 Kgs 18. I began reading in verse 4, "For it came about, when Jezebel destroyed the prophets of the Lord, that Obadiah took a hundred prophets and hid them by fifties in a cave, and provided them with bread and water." After I read this verse in the dream, I awoke.

The following night I had another dream and the Holy Spirit again spoke to me and said, *"I am releasing Obadiah's prophets in the earth. These prophets will have three distinct features to their calling:*

1. *They will be prophets who give themselves to community. I want to put a stop to the wandering prophets. They are not only lonely, but the bitterness and anger in their hearts toward others is destroying the gift that I have given them. I am raising up prophets in the earth that have been fostered in community. Even as the prophets that Obadiah hid in the caves had to learn how*

to live among one another where accountability and checks and balances were a must, I am releasing this very same thing in the earth right now.

2. *The second earmark of these prophets is that they are comfortable in hiding. They do not have a need to be seen and heard. They walk humbly before Me and give their lives to staying out of the spotlight until I release them. Elijah was a showdown prophet, but Obadiah's prophets were lowdown prophets. Many are going to be surprised as these voices, without reputation or finances, carry My words with greater accuracy and timing than many well-known prophets.*

3. *The third earmark of these prophets is that they live on bread and water as their source of life. These prophets will not dine at the table of the world or sit amongst kings. They will work jobs and provide for their families, but they carry the bread of life and water from heaven."*

Then I awoke.

In the days ahead, we need to keep our ears and eyes open for the raising up and sending of Obadiah's prophets in our midst. These prophets will bear the marks of living in community and hold fast to accountability and a system of checks and balances. They will at times travel together and will be directly connected to church leadership. The rise of Obadiah's prophets is going to be a tremendous source of healing, restoration, and relief to shepherds and teachers. These prophets will walk in unusual humility and continually reject the notion of fame and fortune. They will carry the bread of life and water from heaven that can only come from intimacy with the Father.

22

A CULTURE DRIVEN BY HATE

In April of this year, I was in the Dominican Republic observing some missions work there and also gaining insight into the sex-slave trade industry that is occurring in that country.

One night as I went to bed, the Holy Spirit came to me in a dream and said, *"Jeremiah, you must warn those who desire to help sex-trafficking victims to be driven by their love for the victims and not their hate for the predators. You will begin to see many believers very passionate about issues of justice in the days ahead, but warn them about their motives."*

I prophesy that many non-profit organizations that have a heart for sex-trafficking in the days ahead have the potential to be driven by hate, rather than love. Motives of the heart must be searched and placed at the foot of the cross. Even individuals that have a heart for justice to be brought to the unborn must ask themselves, "Am I being driven by a love for the unborn or a hatred for those aborting these babies?" The anti-abortion movement needs a reformation in their thinking on this issue as well.

23

HOMOSEXUAL AND MUSLIM INFLUENCE IN THE MILITARY

In October of this year, I had a dream where I was taken to a military base in the United States and sat amongst high-level army commanders and President Obama. One of the main topics of conversation was on how to allow more homosexual and Islamic faith-based individuals to join the military. President Obama was very excited about this subject and seemed aggressive in his desires to see these two groups be given more power in the military. In particular, there was a high-level military official who was Muslim that Obama favored. As President Obama shared his passion about this to these military officials, I jumped up and pulled the fire alarm.

Then I awoke.

I prophesy that we are going to see the homosexual and Islamic faith-based agenda be welcomed and pushed in the American Military in the days ahead. Meetings and assignments between President Obama and important military officials will take place regarding these two groups.

Jeremiah Johnson

About the Author

Jeremiah Johnson is a graduate of Southeastern University in Lakeland, FL where he earned his bachelors degree in Church Ministries. He entered full time ministry at 20 years old and has had the privilege of traveling and preaching the gospel of Jesus Christ in Africa, India, Israel, and many countries in South and Central America.

He planted Heart of the Father Ministry in 2010 in Lakeland, FL and while carrying a kingdom perspective for life and people, he has continued to minister prophetically to leaders and churches all over the United States and abroad.

Jeremiah's passion is to restore the prophetic ministry to the body of Christ in a way that communicates the Father's Heart and also produces Christ-likeness. He began his prophetic school called "the Samuel Company" in 2008 and has since been used to train and equip thousands of individuals for the prophetic ministry.

Jeremiah is married to his wife Morgan and has two children: Bella Grace and Israel David.

For more information about Heart of the Father Ministry, please visit www.heartofthefatherministry.com.

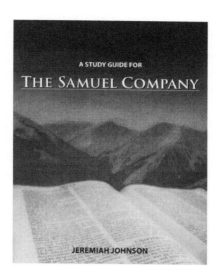

Containing over twelve hours of prophetic training and insight, this CD collection and study guide will teach and encourage you to connect with the character and nature of God as the foundation for all prophetic ministry. There are many who are prophesying the word of the Lord in the body of Christ, but few that are communicating the Father's heart. There is a difference!

Jeremiah Johnson brings fresh revelations and insight into how the prophetic ministry can be released into the local body of believers and how prophetic people can be seen as an asset to pastors and leaders, rather than a liability or a threat.

Visit www.chroniclesoftheunknowndreamer.com to order this cd and/or workbook collection online or call 863-940-2867

Made in the USA
San Bernardino, CA
03 June 2014